MAGIC mud

AND OTHER GREAT EXPERIMENTS

Gordon Penrose

Illustrated by Tina Holdcroft

OWL

Greey de Pencier Books

OWL Books are published in Canada by Greey de Pencier Books, Toronto. OWL is a trademark of the Young Naturalist Foundation.

ISBN 0-920775-18-7

Canadian Cataloguing in Publication Data

Penrose, Gordon, 1925 –
    Magic Mud and other great experiments

ISBN 0-920775-18-7

1. Science—Juvenile literature.
I. Title.

Q163.P295 1987   j500   C87-090111-7

Special thanks to Greg Rist for consulting on several of the activities in this book.

Cover illustration: Rick Jacobsen
Cover and text photography: Tony Thomas
Cover design: Wycliffe Smith

Manufactured in Hong Kong

DEDICATION

To my wife Marion and daughters Lynda, Donna and
Sandra who shared their support for this venture,
To my friend Erle,
To all the people at OWL Magazine for their
challenges and encouragement,
To the children who showed me the joy to be found in
experimenting with everyday things. It is with them
that I share equally my portion of earnings from this
book through charitable organizations that care for
children around the world.

— *Gordon Penrose*

CONTENTS

DR. ZED'S EGG-CITING MAGIC

The Great Egg Challenge #1

How can you tell a raw egg from a hard-boiled egg without cracking the shell?

You can't. It's impossible!

Oh no it's not! It just takes a flick of the wrist.

Huh?

The raw egg keeps spinning because the liquid inside it is still moving.

How to Solve the Great Egg Challenge # 1

1. Spin both eggs on a table.

2. Stop them quickly, then immediately let go of them.

3. One of the eggs will start spinning again when you let it go. Which one?

4

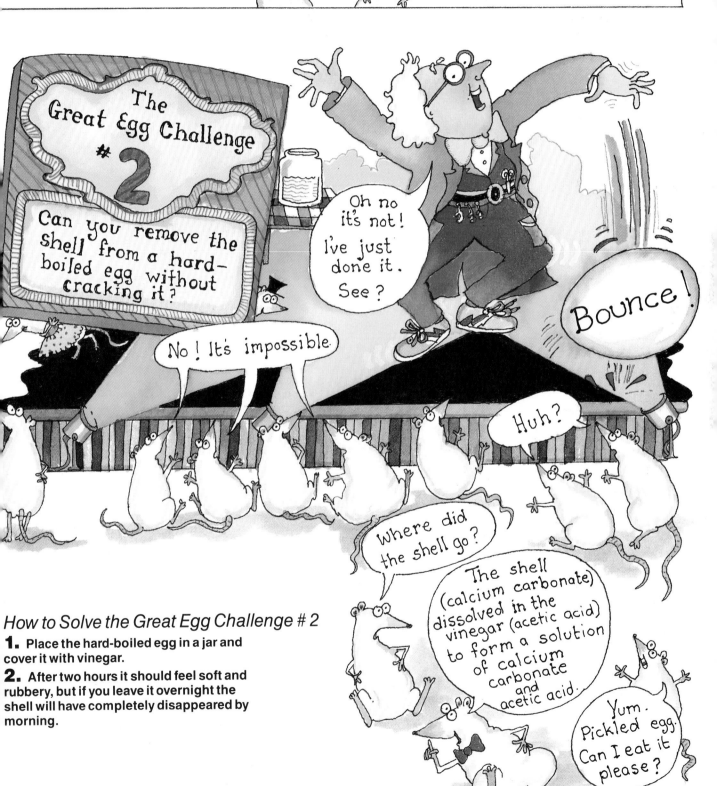

How to Solve the Great Egg Challenge # 2

1. Place the hard-boiled egg in a jar and cover it with vinegar.

2. After two hours it should feel soft and rubbery, but if you leave it overnight the shell will have completely disappeared by morning.

Things you'll need:
thin cardboard; pencil;
scissors

What are ghosts' favourite treats?

Boo-meringues!

Launcher Pattern

How to Make Your Mini-Boomerangs

1. Trace the boomerang and launcher patterns onto the cardboard and cut them out. Fold the launcher along the dotted line.

2. With the launcher held loosely between your thumb and first finger, place one of the arms of a boomerang in it, as shown in the photograph, so the boomerang is just resting at the tip of the launcher.

3. Hold the launcher at about a 45° angle to the ground and flick the tip of the other arm with your first finger.

4. Now try the other shapes or experiment with your own.

Boomerang Pattern

Boomerang Pattern

Boomerang Pattern

Are you sure this thing goes back where it started?

Less torque and more cutting please, Dr. Zed! I want to go next!

Yes! The boomerang's arms turn in opposite directions, creating a force known as torque. This <u>tries</u> to tilt the boomerang but instead makes it turn to one side enough so that the boomerang makes a full circle.

Things you'll need:

75 mL (5 tablespoons) cornstarch;
45 mL (3 tablespoons) water;
measuring spoon; mug, spoon;
food colouring

About this experiment:

Dr. Zed investigates the properties
of a suspension made out of
cornstarch.

How to Make Magic Mud

1. Spoon the cornstarch into the mug.

2. Add the water and stir. It should be difficult to stir, even when the water and cornstarch are fully mixed.

3. Colour your magic mud. N.B. Don't add too much food colouring or your mud will become runny. If this happens, add a little cornstarch until the mud feels like it did in step # 2.

Now Make a Mud Pie

Squeeze a small quantity of magic mud between your fingers and roll it into a ball or sausage. What happens when you stop squeezing the mud?

9

DR. ZED'S ELECTRIC HORSES

How to Make Your Horse

1. Fold the paper in half, and trace the pattern below onto one side of the paper.

2. Holding both halves of the paper together, cut out the pattern, making sure to leave the horse joined together at the top of its head and tail.

3. Decorate both sides of your horse.

Things you'll need:
paper; pencil; scissors; felt-tip pens; hard plastic comb

I'm ecstatic about horses.

They give me quite a charge too!

About this experiment:
Dr. Zed looks at static electricity.

How to Electrify Your Horse

Stand your horse on a smooth surface, comb your hair several times and hold the comb in front of the horse's nose — be sure not to touch the comb to the nose. The horse will move towards the comb. Practise until you can pull the horse along without it ever touching the comb.

As you comb your hair, the comb becomes charged with static electricity.

When you hold the charged comb close to the uncharged paper horse there's a strong attraction between them so the horse races towards the comb.

This is very exciting Sir, but how does it work?

Tina Holdcroft

11

DR. ZED'S FEATHER FLYER

First Make the Body...

1. Fasten the string to the paper clip.

2. Push the paper clip well into the styrofoam ball.

Then Turn it into a Glider...

1. Stick the feathers into opposite sides of the ball. Adjust them so that they both tilt forwards slightly and curve upwards.

2. Run and pull the glider behind you, and it will glide along at about shoulder height.

3. If your glider won't glide properly, experiment with the tilt of its wings.

Those curved feathers really give the flyer a lift.

Yes, their shape helps the air move fast over their top surface. And, as you know, fast-moving air = lower air pressure = lift.

Oh dear, I knew there was some reason I didn't like heights.

Things you'll need:
two large feathers (gull feathers work well); **6 cm (2-1/4 inches) diameter styrofoam ball; paper clip; string; decorations**

Did you know that glider planes use rising, warm air to soar so high?

Big deal! I've been doing that for years.

About this experiment: **Dr. Zed explores Bernoulli's Principle** *(as the speed of a liquid or gas increases, the pressure it exerts decreases).*

change the curve of one feather so that it acts as an air brake, and your feather flyer will spin. What would you do to change your flyer into a kite?

Next Turn it into a Propellor

1. Turn one of the wings so that it curves downwards and remove the string.

2. Climb up on a chair or find a stairwell and drop the feather propellor. It will spin to the ground.

DR. ZED'S JELLY POPS

Things you'll need:

250 mL (1 cup) fruit juice;
15 mL (1 tablespoon) gelatin;
measuring cup and spoon;
small pot; popsicle tray or
small molds; aluminum foil;
popsicle sticks

Did you know that gelatin is a kind of glue that can be made from bones? Slow cooking turns the collagen in bones into gelatin.

Hmmm. Thats why my chicken soup always wobbles in my dish.

About this experiment:

Dr. Zed looks into the reaction of protein molecules in gelatin to heat and cold. (It tastes good too.)

How to Make Jelly Pops

1. To make four jelly pops, pour the juice into the pot and sprinkle the gelatin on it. Stir over low heat until the gelatin dissolves (about five minutes).

2. Rinse out the popsicle tray with cold water then fill it with the juice mixture.

3. Cover the tray with aluminum foil and push a stick through it into each mold.

4. Put the jelly pops into the freezer for about two hours. To remove the pops from the tray, dip the tray into hot water and run a knife blade around the mold edges. Enjoy.

Is he always this weird?

Now that's the tastiest glue I've ever eaten.

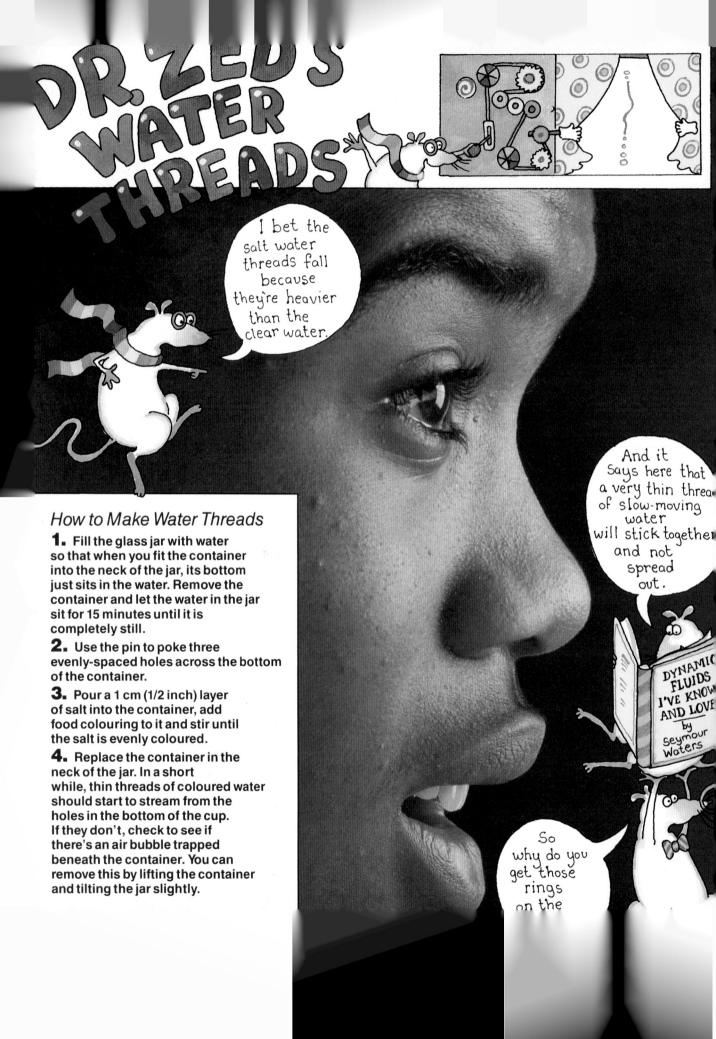

DR. ZED'S WATER THREADS

I bet the salt water threads fall because they're heavier than the clear water.

And it says here that a very thin thread of slow-moving water will stick together and not spread out.

How to Make Water Threads

1. Fill the glass jar with water so that when you fit the container into the neck of the jar, its bottom just sits in the water. Remove the container and let the water in the jar sit for 15 minutes until it is completely still.

2. Use the pin to poke three evenly-spaced holes across the bottom of the container.

3. Pour a 1 cm (1/2 inch) layer of salt into the container, add food colouring to it and stir until the salt is evenly coloured.

4. Replace the container in the neck of the jar. In a short while, thin threads of coloured water should start to stream from the holes in the bottom of the cup. If they don't, check to see if there's an air bubble trapped beneath the container. You can remove this by lifting the container and tilting the jar slightly.

DYNAMIC FLUIDS I'VE KNOWN AND LOVED by Seymour Waters

So why do you get those rings on the

s you'll need:

lass jar; room
rature water; small
container that fits in the
f the jar; pin; salt; food
ng

About this experiment:
Dr. Zed examines fluid dynamics.

DR. ZED'S GREEN SHEEP

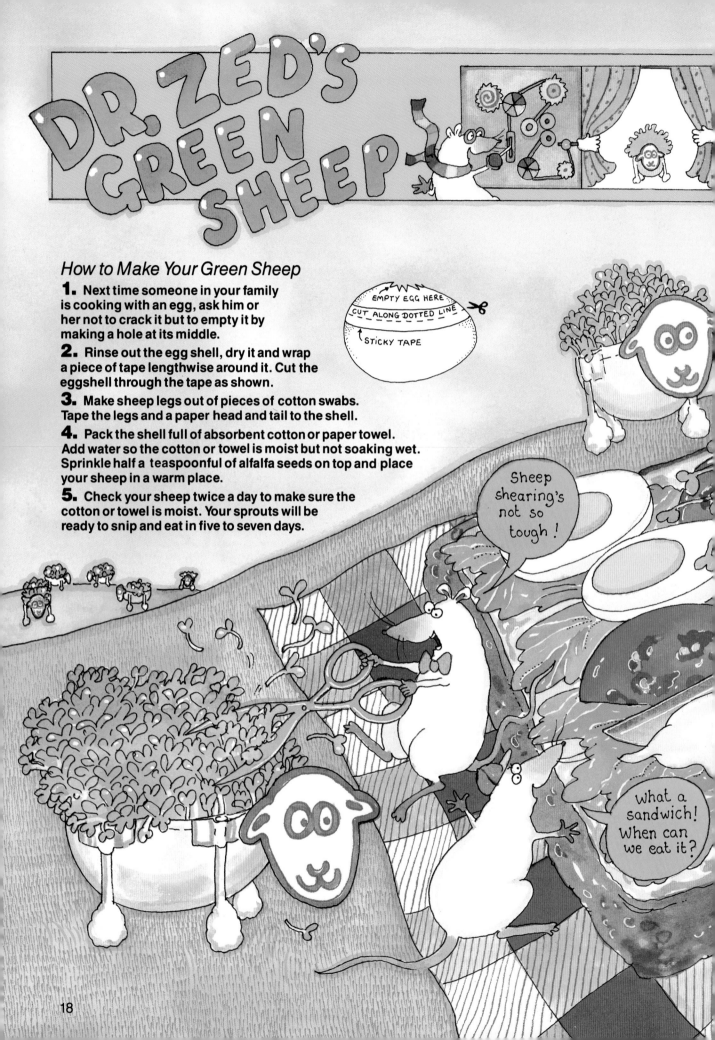

How to Make Your Green Sheep

1. Next time someone in your family is cooking with an egg, ask him or her not to crack it but to empty it by making a hole at its middle.

2. Rinse out the egg shell, dry it and wrap a piece of tape lengthwise around it. Cut the eggshell through the tape as shown.

3. Make sheep legs out of pieces of cotton swabs. Tape the legs and a paper head and tail to the shell.

4. Pack the shell full of absorbent cotton or paper towel. Add water so the cotton or towel is moist but not soaking wet. Sprinkle half a teaspoonful of alfalfa seeds on top and place your sheep in a warm place.

5. Check your sheep twice a day to make sure the cotton or towel is moist. Your sprouts will be ready to snip and eat in five to seven days.

Things you'll need:

stiff cardboard; pencil; ruler; two pocket mirrors loosely taped together on their dull sides; straight pins; disc made out of thin cardboard; felt-tip pens

Did you know the kaleidoscope was invented in 1816 by Sir David Brewster?

About this experiment:

Dr. Zed explores the symmetrical arrangement of images in two mirrors in a see-how-it-works kaleidoscope.

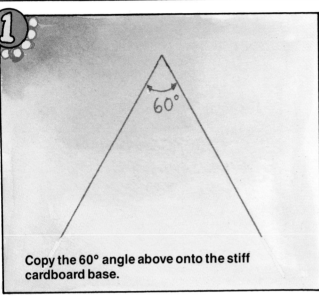

1 Copy the 60° angle above onto the stiff cardboard base.

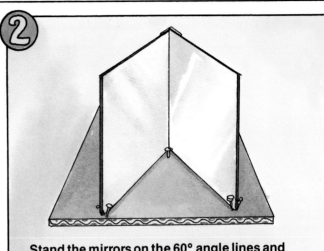

2 Stand the mirrors on the 60° angle lines and stick the pins in place as shown. Lift the mirrors and the centre pin off the base.

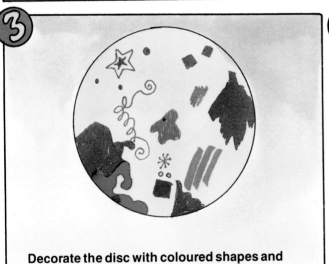

3 Decorate the disc with coloured shapes and patterns.

4 Assemble the kaleidoscope like this:

To make it work, twirl the disc with one hand while holding the base with the other.

Wow! With a 60° angle you get six reflections!

Tina Holdcroft

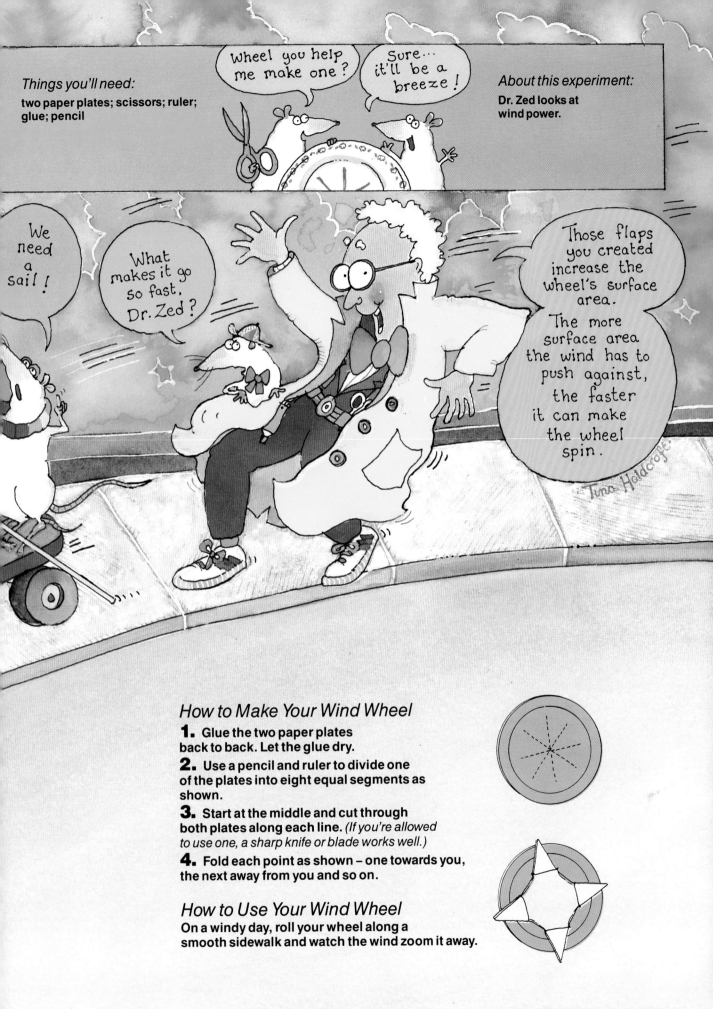

Things you'll need:
two paper plates; scissors; ruler; glue; pencil

Wheel you help me make one?

Sure... it'll be a breeze!

About this experiment:
Dr. Zed looks at wind power.

We need a sail!

What makes it go so fast, Dr. Zed?

Those flaps you created increase the wheel's surface area. The more surface area the wind has to push against, the faster it can make the wheel spin.

Tina Holdcroft

How to Make Your Wind Wheel

1. Glue the two paper plates back to back. Let the glue dry.

2. Use a pencil and ruler to divide one of the plates into eight equal segments as shown.

3. Start at the middle and cut through both plates along each line. *(If you're allowed to use one, a sharp knife or blade works well.)*

4. Fold each point as shown – one towards you, the next away from you and so on.

How to Use Your Wind Wheel

On a windy day, roll your wheel along a smooth sidewalk and watch the wind zoom it away.

Things you'll need:

30 cm x 30 cm (12 inches x 12 inches) square corrugated cardboard; sharp knife; 36 cm x 36 cm x 51 cm (14 inches x 14 inches x 20 inches) triangle brown paper; ruler; decorations

About this experiment:

Dr. Zed examines sound — what it is and how you hear it.

How to Make Your Air Banger

1. Score the front of the cardboard between points A and D, being careful not to cut all the way through. Turn the square over.

2. Place the long side of the paper triangle on the back of the cardboard square between points B and C. Holding the paper in place, flip the square back over *(see diagram)*. Fold the short sides of the paper triangle over the edge of the cardboard and tape them down securely.

3. Fold the cardboard in half along the score line so that the paper folds in half inside it.

4. Decorate your air banger.

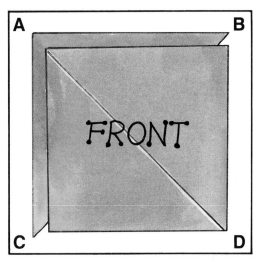

How to Use Your Air Banger

Hold the banger above your head and fling your arm down as hard as you can.

Tina Holdcroft

Things you'll need:
plasticine; cardboard wrapping paper roll; decorations

About this experiment:
Dr. Zed moves a lever's fulcrum point to create an illusion.

can't see any string.

There are no strings attached to this trick! You've simply moved the wand's balance point from the middle by weighting each end differently. This balance point looks impossible but it's where both ends weigh the same.

It looks like magic to me.

How to Make Your Magic Balancing Wand

1. Divide your plasticine into two chunks, one three times bigger than the other.

2. Plug one end of the roll with the small piece of plasticine; plug the other with the large piece.

3. Add a star, if you wish, to the light end of the wand, then find and mark the wand's balance point. Hint: it's closer to the heavy end of the wand than the other.

4. Decorate your wand, making sure that you still know where the balance point is.

How to Do the Trick

1. If you're right-handed, the heavy end of the wand should be on your right side; opposite for left-handers.

2. Balance the wand on your index finger then slowly and gently roll your finger to one side so that the light end of the wand rises.

3. As you wave your free hand over the light end of the wand, give the command, "Rise Up, O Wand of Zed!" and roll your finger so the light end rises. P.S. Practise first!

DR. ZED'S LOVE-IN-YOUR-HEART VALENTINE

How to Make Your Valentine

1. Trace the outline of the two dotted squares and their contents onto the paper.

2. Cut out the two paper squares.

3. Tape one nickel to the top of one side of the cardboard and the other to the bottom of the other side.

4. Tape one paper square to one side of the cardboard. Tape the other one *upside down* on the back of the cardboard.

5. Poke the sharp point of the scissors through the four circles you traced on the paper squares.

6. Cut the string in half. Loop one half through one pair of holes and knot the loose ends together. Do the same with the other half.

Now Put Some Love in Your Heart

1. Hold one loop of string in each hand.

2. Wind up the string by revolving the cardboard.

3. Pull gently on the wound-up string and the cardboard will spin. The word "LOVE" will magically appear between "I" and "YOU" inside the heart.

Aw shucks. How soppy can you get?

28

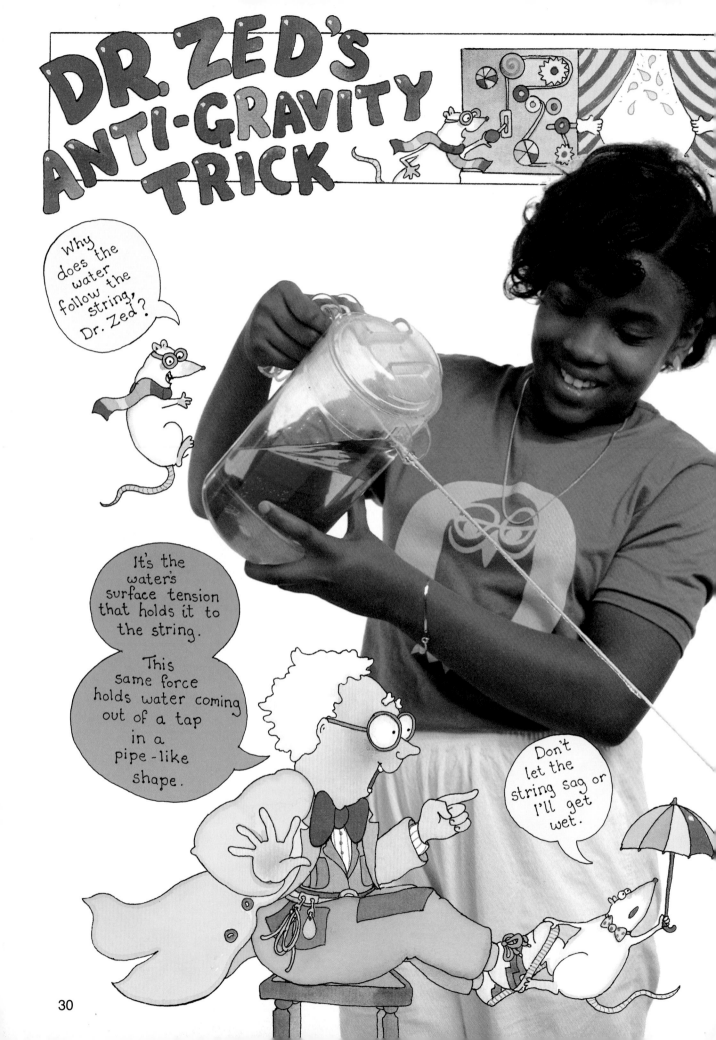

Things you'll need:
plastic measuring jug or pitcher with a handle; plastic cup; piece of string as long as your outstretched arms; water

If you put a blue hat into green water what would it be?

Er, um... turquoise?

Try wet!

About this experiment:
Dr. Zed explores surface tension in water.

How to Set Up the Trick

N.B. Perform this trick where it won't matter if you spill a little water.

1. Wet the string and tie one end of it to the handle of the pitcher.

2. Stretch the string over the spout of the pitcher and let the loose end drop into the cup, which you are holding directly below.

3. Hold the loose end of the string against the inside of the glass so that the string is pulled tight. Carefully begin to pour water into the glass. The water will cling to the string and flow along it into the glass.

How to Defy Gravity

Continue to pour water along the string while you slowly move the cup away from the pitcher. Keep the string tight, don't pour too quickly and the water will follow the string.

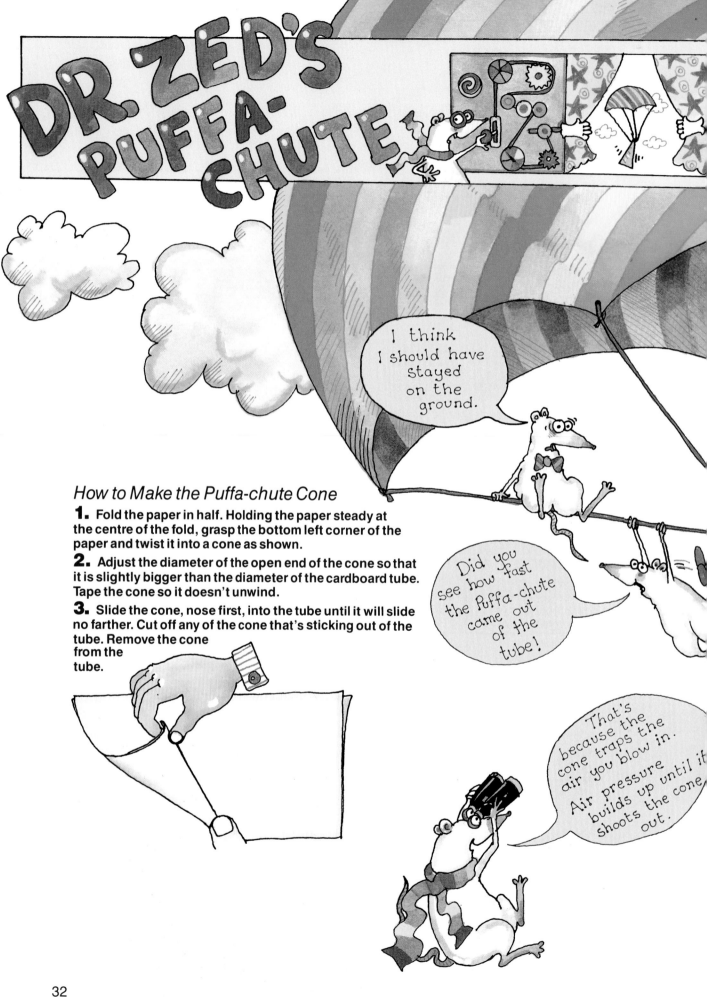

DR. ZED'S PUFFA-CHUTE

I think I should have stayed on the ground.

How to Make the Puffa-chute Cone

1. Fold the paper in half. Holding the paper steady at the centre of the fold, grasp the bottom left corner of the paper and twist it into a cone as shown.

2. Adjust the diameter of the open end of the cone so that it is slightly bigger than the diameter of the cardboard tube. Tape the cone so it doesn't unwind.

3. Slide the cone, nose first, into the tube until it will slide no farther. Cut off any of the cone that's sticking out of the tube. Remove the cone from the tube.

Did you see how fast the Puffa-chute came out of the tube!

That's because the cone traps the air you blow in. Air pressure builds up until it shoots the cone out.

About this experiment:

Dr. Zed looks at air pressure as well as the effects of air resistance on a large surface.

How to Launch Your Puffa-chute

1. Slide the cone, open end first, into the cardboard tube until none of it is sticking out.

2. Place the loaded end of the tube in the centre of the chute and gather the ends of the chute around the tube.

3. As you blow hard into the open end of the tube, let go of the plastic chute.

How to Make the Plastic Chute

1. Cut a 24 cm x 24 cm (9-1/2 inches x 9-1/2 inches) square out of the plastic bag.

2. Cut four threads 24 cm (9-1/2 inches) long and tie one to each corner of the plastic square.

3. Knot the four loose ends of thread together and tape to the nose of the paper cone.

33

Did you know that 16 million million million atoms rush to join a sugar crystal every hour?

That's what I call a rush-hour!

About this experiment:

Dr. Zed examines crystal formation in a supersaturated sugar solution.

How to Make Your Crystal Pops

1. Mix the sugar and water in the pot and heat it on the stove, stirring until the sugar dissolves. Boil the mixture for one minute.

2. Take the pot off the stove. When the mixture is cool, pour it into the glass or jar.

3. Put a popsicle stick in the jar and leave it uncovered in a warm room until large crystals start to form. This will take about a week.

If a crust forms, break it and gather the floating crystals on to your popsicle stick.

I'm impressed. When can I eat it?

Go back to sleep. We'll wake you when it's ready. Tee hee.

Tina Holdcroft

35

DR. ZED'S SEE-ALL CAT'S EYES

Tab A

Eye strip

SLIT A

Cut out. dotted circle

Cut out dotted circle

Tab B

How to Make Your See-All Cat's Eyes:

1. Trace and colour the cat's face and the eye strip next to it. Cut along slits A and B.

2. Working from the back of the cat's face, push tab A through slit A, and tab B through slit B.

3. When you turn the face over you should see eyes in the circles and there should be a space between the eye strip and the back of the face.

4. Hang the cat's face at eye level, then move at least 3 m (10 feet) away. As you walk about, watch what the cat's eyes do.

Run! It's a cat!

Things you'll need:
paper; felt-tip pens;
scissors; thread and tape to
hang the cat's face

Why do witches fly on brooms?

Because vacuum cleaners are too heavy!

About this experiment:
Dr. Zed investigates optical illusions created by objects on different planes and seen from different angles.

It can't be watching all of us! What's happening, Dr. Zed?

No! No! It's watching me!

It's watching me!

When you move to one side of the cat, the eyeholes frame a different section of the continuous eyestrip, making the pupils appear to turn towards you.

But you were the only one that moved.

...Tina Holdcroft...

37

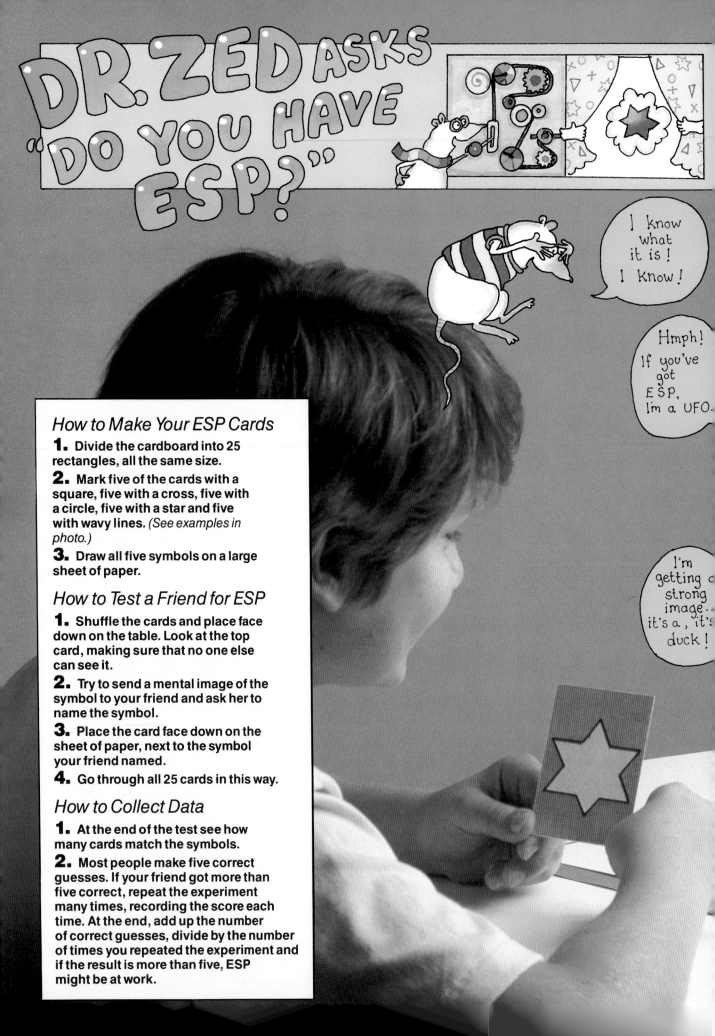

DR. ZED ASKS "DO YOU HAVE ESP?"

I know what it is! I know!

Hmph! If you've got ESP, I'm a UFO.

I'm getting a strong image.. it's a, it's a duck!

How to Make Your ESP Cards

1. Divide the cardboard into 25 rectangles, all the same size.

2. Mark five of the cards with a square, five with a cross, five with a circle, five with a star and five with wavy lines. *(See examples in photo.)*

3. Draw all five symbols on a large sheet of paper.

How to Test a Friend for ESP

1. Shuffle the cards and place face down on the table. Look at the top card, making sure that no one else can see it.

2. Try to send a mental image of the symbol to your friend and ask her to name the symbol.

3. Place the card face down on the sheet of paper, next to the symbol your friend named.

4. Go through all 25 cards in this way.

How to Collect Data

1. At the end of the test see how many cards match the symbols.

2. Most people make five correct guesses. If your friend got more than five correct, repeat the experiment many times, recording the score each time. At the end, add up the number of correct guesses, divide by the number of times you repeated the experiment and if the result is more than five, ESP might be at work.

About this experiment:
Dr. Zed examines how proteins
react to the stress of being mixed
and heated.

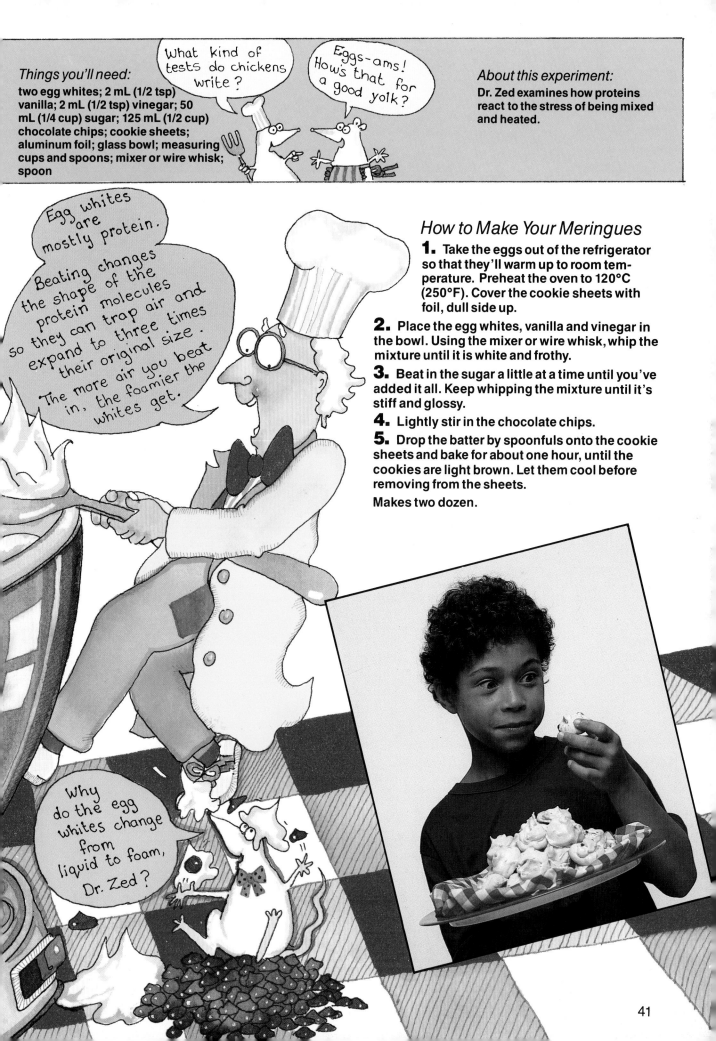

How to Make Your Meringues

1. Take the eggs out of the refrigerator
so that they'll warm up to room tem-
perature. Preheat the oven to 120°C
(250°F). Cover the cookie sheets with
foil, dull side up.

2. Place the egg whites, vanilla and vinegar in
the bowl. Using the mixer or wire whisk, whip the
mixture until it is white and frothy.

3. Beat in the sugar a little at a time until you've
added it all. Keep whipping the mixture until it's
stiff and glossy.

4. Lightly stir in the chocolate chips.

5. Drop the batter by spoonfuls onto the cookie
sheets and bake for about one hour, until the
cookies are light brown. Let them cool before
removing from the sheets.

Makes two dozen.

How to Make Your Moving Mouse Machine

1. Mark cardboard like this:

10 cm (4 inches)

3.5 cm (1-3/8 inch)

Each slot is 5 cm (2 inches) long, 6 cm (1/4 inch) wide and 6 cm (1/4 inch) from the top. Cut 10.

.6 cm (1/4 inch) tab for gluing

35.5 cm (14 inches)

2. Ask an adult to help you cut out the 10 slots.

Tab

Things you'll need:

35.5 cm x 10 cm (14 inches x 4 inches) rectangle thin cardboard; scissors; **sharp knife** (*ask permission to use this*); **pencil; ruler; tracing paper; paper; glue; turntable**

Did you know that Dr. Zed's moving mouse machine was invented more than 150 years ago?

Really? He doesn't look that old!

About this experiment:

Dr. Zed explores persistence of vision.

Not moving? What does he mean, Dr. Zed?

He's right! Your brain continues to see each picture one-tenth of a second after it's disappeared. Since the cylinder is turning quickly, your brain overlaps the images so it looks as if the mouse is somersaulting.

3. Trace the two strips of mouse drawings below. Join the strips together to form a continuous loop with the mouse drawings inside.

4. Assemble the moving mouse machine so that it looks like this:

Lights, Camera, Action...

Stand your moving mouse machine on the turntable, making sure that it's centred. Switch on the turntable to 33 rpm and look through the slots so you can see the revolving pictures.
Can you see the mouse flip?

Tab

43

DR. ZED'S SATELLITE BALLOON

This is some spaced-out experiment!

Aw, admit it, Dr. Zed, you glued these cups on, didn't you?

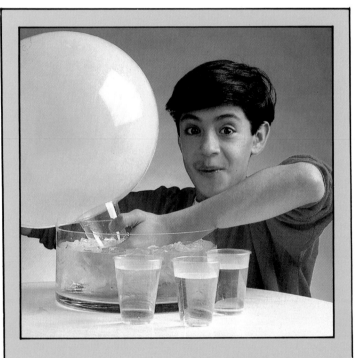

How to Make Your Satellite Balloon

1. Blow up the balloon and knot it.

2. Fill a large basin with cold water and ice.

3. Fill several plastic cups with the hottest water you can get out of the tap. Watch your fingers!

4. Empty out one cup into the sink. Quickly press the open end of the cup against the balloon.

5. Holding the cup firmly against the balloon, immediately dip the cup into the basin of ice water. Hold it there 20 seconds.

6. Let go of the cup and it will stay in place.

7. Stick on as many cups as you can in this way.

N.B. If you can't get your cup to stick to the balloon, either the water isn't hot or cold enough or you're not working fast enough.

Things you'll need:
large, round balloon; plastic cups; hot and cold water; large basin; ice; string for hanging the balloon

About this experiment:
Dr. Zed shows how to create a partial vacuum by the rapid cooling of hot air.

Bet you can't name the biggest satellite orbiting the earth.

That's easy! The moon!

No I didn't. The cups stick because the rapidly cooled air inside them takes up less space than when it was hot.

This creates less air pressure in the cups than in the balloon, so the balloon pushes up into each cup and "grabs" hold of it.

45

DATE:	EXPERIMENT:

NOTES:

Index

ABOUT THE AUTHOR

Gordon Penrose, the zany Dr. Zed, is regularly featured in OWL, the international magazine for children, and on OWL/TV, the childrens' discovery program broadcast throughout North America. A retired Master Teacher of Science, Gordon now travels extensively, giving science workshops for children and educators. This is his third science activity book.

Dr. Zed's philosophy, like that of OWL Magazine, is that learning can be fun. Because it is important for children to discover for themselves, all the activities in this book encourage creative experimentation, and while each one focuses on one major science understanding, it touches on others as well. All the activities have been tested with children, can be carried out with a minimum of adult supervision, and are designed to be suitable for both home and classroom.